Contents

Any words appearing in the text in bold, **like this**,
are explained in the Glossary.

The seasons

In some parts of the world, the **year** consists of two seasons – a dry season and a rainy season. In central Australia, the Aborigines divide their year into five seasons. For most of us, though, the year is made up of four seasons: **spring**, **summer**, **autumn** and **winter**.

The importance of the seasons

The things we do are influenced by the seasons. This was particularly true in the past when more people worked on the land. In spring, new lambs are born. Towards the end of the summer, wheat, corn and other crops are harvested. In the autumn and winter, the fields are ploughed and made ready for replanting.

Lambs are born in the spring.

The Greenwich Guide to the
Seasons

Graham Dolan

Royal Observatory Greenwich

www.heinemann.co.uk
Visit our website to find out more information about Heinemann Library books.

To order:
 Phone 44 (0) 1865 888066
 Send a fax to 44 (0) 1865 314091
Visit the Heinemann Bookshop at www.heinemann.co.uk to browse our catalogue
and order online.

First published in Great Britain by Heinemann Library, Halley Court, Jordan Hill, Oxford OX2 8EJ, a division of Reed Educational and Professional Publishing Ltd. Heinemann is a registered trademark of Reed Educational & Professional Publishing Ltd.

OXFORD MELBOURNE AUCKLAND JOHANNESBURG BLANTYRE
GABORONE IBADAN PORTSMOUTH (NH) USA CHICAGO

Designed by Celia Floyd
Illustrations by Jeff Edwards
Originated by Dot Gradations, UK
Printed in Hong Kong/China

05 04 03 02 01
10 9 8 7 6 5 4 3 2 1
ISBN 0 431 13001 9

British Library Cataloguing in Publication Data

Dolan, Graham
  The Greenwich Guide to the seasons
  1. Seasons – Juvenile literature
  I. Title II. The seasons
  525.5

Acknowledgements
The Publishers would like to thank the following for permission to reproduce photographs: Pg.4 Still Pictures; Pg.5 PhotoDisc; Pg.12 National Maritime Museum; Pg.13 National Maritime Museum; Pg.19 Oxford Scientific Films; Pg.20 NHPA; Pg.21 Bruce Coleman Collection; Pg.22 Oxford Scientific Films; Pg.23 [top] Bruce Coleman Collection [bottom] Oxford Scientific Films; Pg.24 Science Photo Library; Pg.25 Science Photo Library; Pg.26 Oxford Scientific films; Pg.27 Oxford Scientific Films; Pg 28 Bruce Coleman Collection; Pg.29 Bruce Coleman Collection.

Cover photograph reproduced with permission of PhotoDisc.

Spine logo reproduced with permission of the National Maritime Museum.

Every effort has been made to contact copyright holders of any material reproduced in this book. Any omissions will be rectified in subsequent printings if notice is given to the Publisher.

When we go on holiday, what we do, and where we go, often depends on the time of year. We usually go on beach holidays in the summer, when the weather is warmer. Skiing holidays are usually taken in the winter, when the weather is colder and there is snow on the ground.

Summer holidays at the seaside.

But why do the seasons occur? And why are they repeated from one year to the next? Why is it summer in Australia when it is winter in Europe and North America? The answers to these questions lie in the way in which the Earth **orbits** the Sun.

5

Our moving Earth

The Sun is our nearest star. It gives us light and **energy**. The Earth moves around the Sun. This movement, or **orbit**, affects our **years**, seasons and **days**.

As the Earth goes on its journey, we pass from one season to the next. The pattern of the seasons repeats itself each time the Earth begins a new orbit. Our year is based on this repeating pattern. The pattern repeats itself roughly every $365\frac{1}{4}$ days.

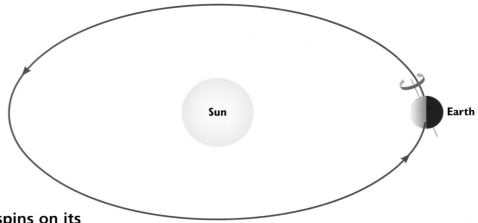

The Earth spins on its axis just over 365 times in the time that it takes to orbit the Sun once.

Day and night

Our Earth is also spinning on its own **axis**. When the part of the Earth that we are on faces the Sun, we receive light and energy. We call it **daytime**. As the Earth spins, we eventually end up facing away from the Sun. When this happens, light and energy from the Sun can no longer reach us. It goes dark and night begins.

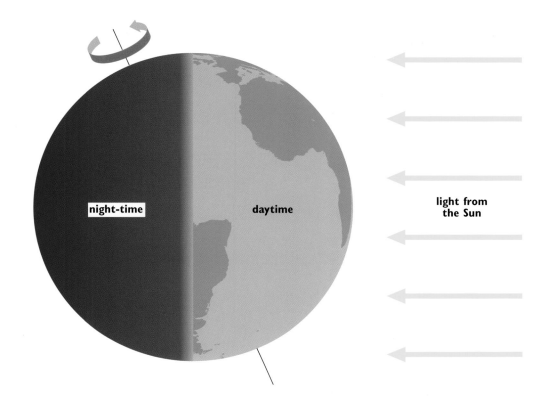

night-time

daytime

light from
the Sun

**When it is daytime
on one side of the Earth,
it is night-time on the other.**

Long and short days

We say that the days in **winter** are shorter than they are in **summer**, but we don't mean that the days themselves are shorter. Each day is always 24 hours long. Instead, we mean that there are fewer hours of daylight each day and more hours of darkness. This happens because the Earth leans as it orbits the Sun.

Our leaning Earth

As the Earth makes its journey around the Sun, it leans at an angle. This affects the length of our **days** and the height at which the Sun appears in the sky. It causes the seasons to occur.

As the Earth moves around its **orbit**, the direction in which it leans scarcely changes. On one side of its orbit, around June, the Earth's North Pole points towards the Sun. On the opposite side of its orbit, around December, the North Pole points away from the Sun.

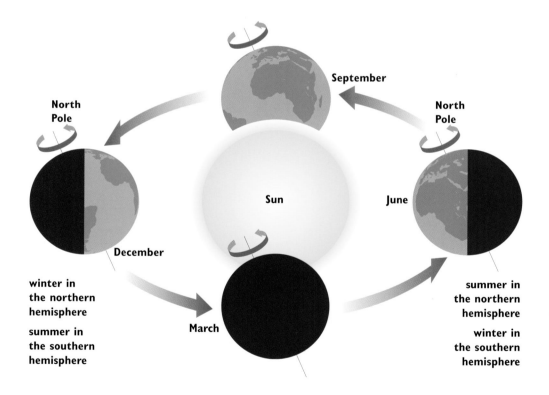

September

North
Pole

North
Pole

Sun

June

December

winter in
the northern
hemisphere

summer in
the southern
hemisphere

March

summer in
the northern
hemisphere

winter in
the southern
hemisphere

**The Earth always leans in the
same direction as it orbits the Sun.**

Summer and winter

When the North Pole points towards the Sun, people north of the **tropics** get warmer weather – they have their **summer**. When it points away from the Sun, they get colder weather – they have their **winter**.

When the North Pole points towards the Sun, there are more hours of daylight each day, and the Sun rises higher in the sky. More **energy** is received and it is hotter.

In countries south of the tropics, summer occurs when the South Pole points towards the Sun. This happens when the North Pole is pointing away from the Sun.

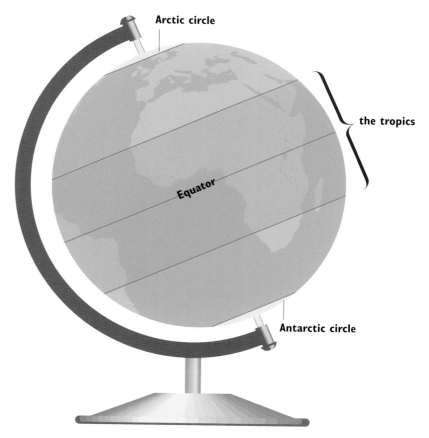

The tropics cover the areas of the Earth on either side of the Equator.

The effect of the Earth's lean

The changing length of the day

In Britain the **days** are longer in the **summer**, because the Earth is leaning on its **axis**. This part of the Earth, in the **northern hemisphere**, spends more of the day facing towards the Sun than facing away from it. When days are longer, the Earth receives more **energy** from the Sun, and the weather is hotter. In **winter** this part of the Earth spends more of the day facing away from the Sun than towards it. It receives less energy, and the weather is colder.

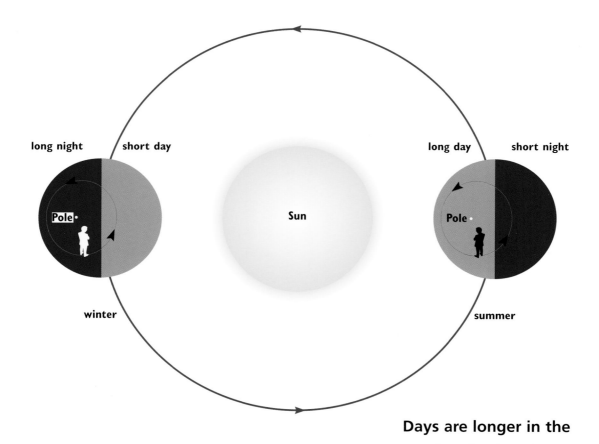

Days are longer in the summer than in the winter.

The height of the Sun

It also gets hotter in the summer because the Sun rises higher in the sky. This too is an effect caused by the Earth leaning on its axis. In summer, when the Sun rises high in the sky, the Sun's energy shines directly on the Earth. The Earth's surface gets lots of strong sunshine and **temperatures** are warm. In winter, when the Sun is lower in the sky, its energy is spread out over a larger area of the Earth's surface. It gets less sunshine and the temperature is colder.

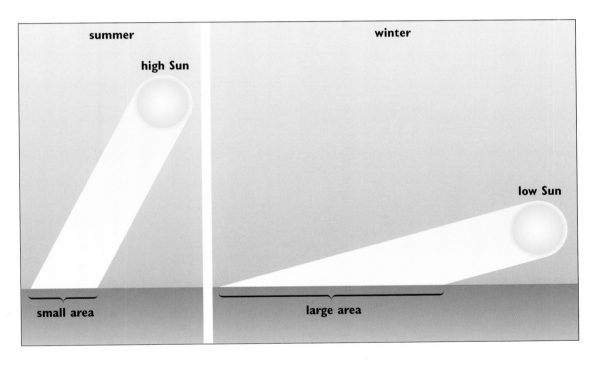

The **midday** Sun appears much higher in the sky in the summer than in the winter. When the Sun is lower, its energy is spread over a greater area – we get less of it, and the weather is colder.

The four seasons

Winter

In **winter**, the **midday** Sun is low in the sky. It is the time of **year** when **temperatures** are usually at their lowest. During the winter **months**, many trees are leafless and some animals **hibernate**.

In some places snow is common in the winter. In others it is much rarer.

Spring

In temperate areas, the appearance of daffodils marks the start of spring.

As the Earth continues its journey around the Sun, the **days** rapidly become longer, and the Sun rises higher in the sky. Little by little it starts to get warmer and **spring** begins. The buds on trees start to open, and new leaves appear. Birds lay their eggs, which hatch a few weeks later.

Summer

In the **summer** the days are at their longest, and the midday Sun is at its highest. Crops in the fields begin to ripen and young birds leave their nests.

Autumn

In the **autumn** the days quickly start to get shorter. The Sun does not rise so high in the sky, and the temperature begins to fall. Wild animals prepare themselves for the winter that will follow. The leaves of **deciduous trees** change colour and fall to the ground.

13

The length of our day

The length of our **day** depends on where we are and the time of **year**. On the **Equator**, every day of the year has almost equal amounts of **daytime** and **night-time**.

The further north or south of the Equator you are, the greater the difference between the amount of daytime in the **summer** and the amount of daytime in the **winter**.

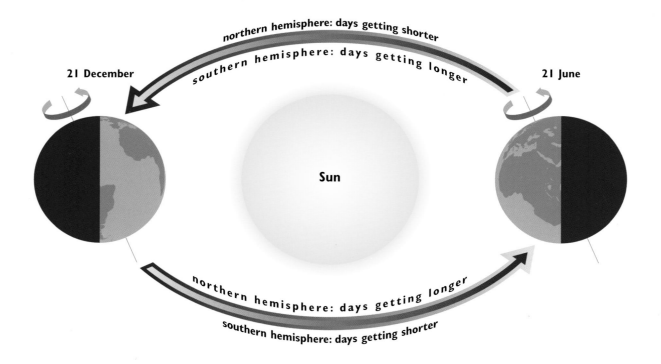

northern hemisphere: days getting shorter

southern hemisphere: days getting longer

21 December

21 June

Sun

northern hemisphere: days getting longer

southern hemisphere: days getting shorter

The length of our days changes
as the Earth **orbits** the Sun.

The path of the Sun at different times of the year from London. It moves in a similar way in the USA and most of Europe.

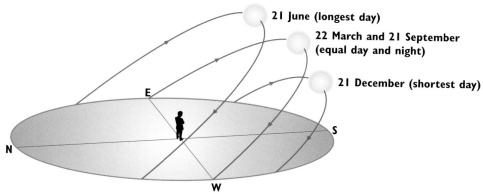

21 June (longest day)

22 March and 21 September (equal day and night)

21 December (shortest day)

The longest and shortest days

The **longest** and **shortest days** of the year occur in June and December. The amount of daylight increases each day between the shortest and the longest day. It then starts to decrease again. Roughly half-way between the two, we get more or less equal amounts of daytime and night-time.

length of day	approximate date	
	northern hemisphere (USA, UK)	southern hemisphere (Australia)
longest day	21 June	21 December
shortest day	21 December	21 June
equal day and night	22 September and 21 March	21 March and 22 September

The seasons in the Arctic and Antarctic

The land of the midnight Sun

In the **Arctic** and **Antarctic** circles, around the North and South Poles, there are long periods of unbroken darkness during the **winter**. In the **summer**, the Sun is still in the sky at midnight. There are long periods of continuous daylight. At the Poles, there is about half a **year** of continuous **night-time** followed by half a year of uninterrupted **daytime**. The number of **days** of each gets less as you move away from the Poles.

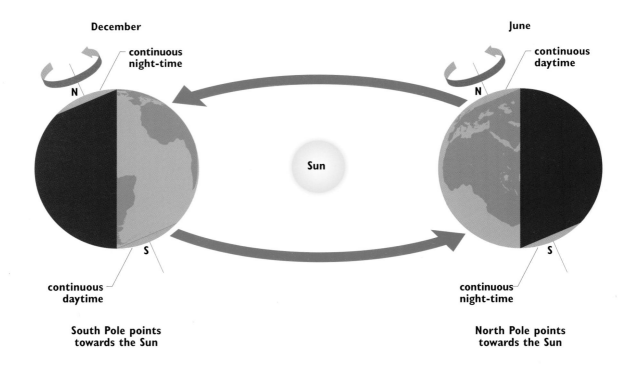

December

continuous night-time

N

Sun

S

continuous daytime

South Pole points towards the Sun

June

continuous daytime

N

S

continuous night-time

North Pole points towards the Sun

The land of the midnight Sun.

The circling polar Sun

At the Poles, the Sun moves round and round the sky at virtually the same height from one day to the next. It moves in a spiral. At the North Pole, it spirals continuously upwards until about 21 June. It then starts to spiral downwards again.

**The upward path of the Sun
at the North Pole in May.**

The South Pole

At the South Pole the average temperature in December (in the summer) is minus 28° Celsius – colder than an ordinary freezer! Even so, it is 30° Celsius higher than the average temperature in June (in the winter), which is minus 58° Celsius.

The seasons near the Equator

The absence of seasons

The four seasons, **spring**, **summer**, **autumn** and **winter**, don't occur near the **Equator**. There is very little difference in temperature from one **month** of the **year** to the next. This is because each **day** is about the same length and the **midday** Sun is always high in the sky.

location		average temperature (°Celsius)	
		highest month	lowest month
Equator	London		
Equator	Singapore		
Equator	Sydney		

Rainy and dry seasons

In some places in the **tropics**, there is a dry and a rainy season. Part of the year is drier than normal, and part of the year is wetter. In other parts of the tropics, the rain falls more evenly throughout the year. The type of **climate** is influenced by the heating and cooling of the nearby land and oceans.

In the tropical rainforest, rain normally falls throughout the year.

height of midday Sun		*amount of daytime and night-time*	
highest	lowest	**longest day**	**shortest day**

Deciduous and evergreen trees

In the **tropics**, trees usually keep their leaves all through the **year**. Trees like this are called **evergreen trees**. Many of them have broad (wide) leaves. Beyond the tropics, there is usually a mixture of evergreen and **deciduous trees**. Deciduous trees normally lose all their leaves in the **autumn**, and grow new ones in the **spring**.

Autumn colours

The leaves of deciduous trees change colour before they fall to the ground in the autumn. The colour they turn depends on the type of tree. Some turn red. Others turn yellow or brown. The brightness of the colours is affected by the **summer** and autumn weather. New England in the USA is famous for its autumn colours.

The leaves of deciduous trees change colour before they are lost in autumn.

Evergreens in cold countries

The evergreen trees found in very cold places are usually **conifers**. Their leaves look like thin spiky needles. Although evergreens with broad leaves are often able to survive in the warmer **winters** in the UK, most are unable to survive the colder winters of the northern USA and Canada.

Woodland plants

Plants need light to grow. The ground in deciduous woodlands receives most light in the early spring when the trees have no leaves. This is when many woodland plants flower. In the summer, when there is a leaf **canopy** overhead, it is darker. Many woodland plants die back, surviving beneath the ground until growth starts again in the autumn.

Bluebells are woodland flowers. They flower in late spring.

Hibernation and migration

Hibernation

In the **winter** there is less food around for wild animals. Some mammals survive the cold winters and the reduction in food supply by **hibernating**. In the **autumn**, when food supplies are plentiful, they fatten themselves up and build up an **energy** store. When they hibernate they find a cosy place to settle for the winter. Their body **temperature** and heart-rate drops. They use energy at a slower rate, and are able to use their stored energy to live through the winter. To an outsider, they look as though they are asleep.

Dormice hibernate in the winter.

Migration

Some birds fly to a warmer country for the winter. This is called **migration**. Swallows, for example, spend the **summer** in northern Europe and the winter thousands of kilometres away in Africa, where it is warmer.

Fur colour and length

In the winter, when it is colder, mammals – for example cats – grow more and longer hair. In the summer, when it is warmer, they lose hair. This is called **moulting**. The colour of the fur of some mammals also changes with the seasons. This helps them to stay **camouflaged** as the landscape around them changes.

Stoats (in winter they are called called ermine) have brown fur in the summer, but white fur in the winter.

23

The seasons on other planets

Most of the planets have seasons. The more a planet leans on its **axis**, the greater the difference between its **summer** and **winter**. The planet that leans the most is Uranus. It is almost lying on its side. The planet that leans the least is Mercury. Mars and Earth both lean at about the same angle.

Uranus spins on its side, causing a big difference between its summers and winters. The blue-green colour is caused by methane gas in its atmosphere.

planet	tilt of axis (°)
Mercury	0
Venus	3
Earth	23
Mars	25
Jupiter	3
Saturn	27
Uranus	82
Neptune	28
Pluto	56

Surface temperatures

Many other factors also affect the **climate** and weather patterns on the planets. These include the amount and type of **atmosphere** and the distance from the Sun. In general, the further a planet is from the Sun, the colder its surface **temperature**.

Small planets have less **gravity** and less atmosphere than larger ones. Mercury, the smallest of the inner planets, has almost no atmosphere. Venus is about the same size as Earth and has an atmosphere made up mainly of carbon dioxide. Carbon dioxide is a greenhouse gas. This means that it traps the Sun's **energy** and makes the planet hotter.

The surface of Venus is permanently covered in clouds.

As a result, the surface temperature on Venus is higher than on Mercury, even though it is further from the Sun. Mercury does not lean on its axis. All its days are the same length, and there are no seasons.

What if...?

... the Earth was closer to the Sun?

If the Earth was closer to the Sun, we would still get the seasons, but it would be hotter. The Earth would **orbit** the Sun more quickly. Our **years** would be shorter, and so too would each of our seasons.

If we were close enough to the Sun, it would be too warm for water to freeze in the **winter**. The ice-caps of the **Arctic** and **Antarctic** would not have formed and the sea levels would be higher. If we were closer still, it would be too hot for life as we know it to exist.

If the Earth was closer to the Sun, the ice-caps would not exist.

If the Earth didn't lean, there would be no deciduous trees. Trees would keep their leaves throughout the year because the **temperature** would be about the same in December as in June.

... the Earth didn't lean?

If the Earth didn't lean we wouldn't get our seasons. And if we didn't have the seasons, we probably wouldn't measure time in years either. Our longest unit of time would be the **month**. The length of each month is based on the time it takes for the Moon to orbit the Earth.

If there were no seasons, there would be no **deciduous trees**. All the trees would be **evergreens**.

If the Earth didn't lean, the **midday** Sun would always reach the same height in the sky. Each **day** would be much like any other day. Every day would have virtually equal amounts of **daytime** and **night-time**. The further away from the **Equator** you were, the cooler it would be.

Factfile

Long school holidays in the **summer** are a hangover from the **days** when children helped to collect the harvest.

The highest **temperature** ever recorded (in the shade) on the Earth's surface was 58° Celsius. The lowest was minus 89.2° Celsius.

In Verkhoyansk in Russia, the difference between the highest recorded summer temperature and the lowest recorded **winter** temperature is 105° Celsius. This is greater than the difference in temperature between freezing and boiling water.

In Murmansk, the largest Russian town inside the **Arctic** Circle, the Sun doesn't set for about 62 days in a row in the summer.

Arctic ground squirrels **hibernate** for nine **months** of the year.

Arctic ground squirrel.

The coldest place where people live all through the year is the village of Oymyakon in Russia, where the temperature has fallen below minus 70° Celsius.

Nearly one-tenth of the Earth's land is permanently covered in ice. It stays frozen even in the summer months.

Around 21 March and 22 September, the **midday** Sun passes directly overhead at the **Equator**.

The seasons on Mars last roughly twice as long as those on Earth. Mars is further from the Sun, so it takes longer to complete each orbit.

Once a tree has been cut down, its age can be worked out by counting the number of tree rings – one for each **year** of its life. The rings are formed because trees grow at different rates in different seasons.

Garden plants which are able to survive the cold weather and frosts in winter are called hardy plants.

The body temperature of snakes and other reptiles is higher in the summer than in the winter.

Tree rings.

Glossary

Antarctic the part of the Earth near the South Pole

Arctic the part of the Earth near the North Pole

atmosphere a layer of gases that surrounds a planet. A planet's atmosphere affects its temparature and weather.

autumn the season between summer and winter

axis an imaginary line passing through the centre of a planet from the North to the South pole, around which the planet spins

camouflage to blend in with the surrounding area, often by changing colour

canopy a covering of something

climate the general type of weather and temperatures that a place experiences

conifer a tree like a pine or fir tree that is evergreen and has needles and cones

day a length of time based on the time it takes for the Earth to spin round once on its axis

daytime the time between sunrise and sunset

deciduous tree a tree that loses all its leaves in the autumn and grows new ones in the spring

energy what it takes to heat something up or to make it move

Equator an imaginary line that separates the Earth's northern and southern hemispheres

evergreen tree a tree that keeps its leaves throughout the year

gravity a force that attracts objects to each other. The Earth's gravity gives us our weight.

hibernate to spend the winter in an inactive state

longest day the day in the year with the most hours and minutes of daytime

midday the time when the Sun reaches its highest point of the day

migrate to move from one place to another

month a length of time based on the time it takes for the Moon to orbit the Earth once

moulting the shedding of hair in the spring and summer

night-time the time between sunset and sunrise

northern hemisphere the half of the Earth north of the Equator – the top half of a globe

orbit the path of a planet around the Sun or a moon around a planet

shortest day the day in the year with the fewest hours and minutes of daytime

southern hemisphere the half of the Earth south of the Equator – the bottom half of a globe

spring the season between winter and summer

summer the hottest part of the year when the days are longest and the Sun rises highest in the sky

temperature how hot or cold something is

tropics the part of the Earth near the Equator

winter the coldest part of the year when the days are shortest and the Sun is always low in the sky

year a length of time based on the time taken for the Earth to orbit the Sun once and for the cycle of seasons to repeat itself. A normal calendar year has 365 days. A leap year has 366 days.

Index

5707

Contents

Any words appearing in the text in bold, **like this,** are explained in the glossary. You can also look out for them in the Star words box at the bottom of each page.

Who is the real Johnny Depp?

Johnny Depp has played many roles. He has been a pirate, a detective, and a writer – to name just a few of his many screen characters. So what is the real Johnny like?

ALL ABOUT JOHNNY

Full name: John Christopher Depp II
Born: 9 June 1963
Place of birth: Owensboro, Kentucky, USA
Family: Father: John, Mother: Betty Sue, Brother: Dan, Half-sisters: Debbie and Christie
Height: 5 feet 10 inches (1.77 metres)
Relationships: Married Lori Allison (1983–1985). Lived with Sherilyn Fenn, Jennifer Grey, Winona Ryder, and Kate Moss. Now lives with Vanessa Paradis (1998–)
Children: Lily-Rose Melody (born 1999), John Christopher Depp III – known as Jack (born 2002)
Big break: Appearing as a detective, Tommy Hanson, in the US television series *21 Jump Street* (1987)
Interests: Playing guitar, collecting things, hanging out with his family

> " I do what I want. I won't be a slave to success. "

Johnny likes to play unusual roles such as Edward Scissorhands.

Star words   director   person in charge of making a film

STAR ★ FILES

Johnny Depp

Jane Bingham

www.raintreepublishers.co.uk
Visit our website to find out more information about **Raintree** books.

To order:
☎ Phone 44 (0) 1865 888113
🖹 Send a fax to 44 (0) 1865 314091
🖥 Visit the Raintree Bookshop at **www.raintreepublishers.co.uk** to browse our catalogue and order online.

Produced for Raintree by
White-Thomson Publishing Ltd
Bridgewater Business Centre
210 High Street, Lewes, BN7 2NH

First published in Great Britain by Raintree,
Halley Court, Jordan Hill, Oxford OX2 8EJ,
part of Harcourt Education.
Raintree is a registered trademark of
Harcourt Education Ltd.

© Harcourt Education Ltd 2005
The moral right of the proprietor has
been asserted.

Editorial: Catherine Clarke, Sarah Shannon
and Kate Buckingham
Design: Leishman Design and Michelle Lisseter
Picture Research: Catherine Clarke
Production: Chloe Bloom

Originated by Modern Age
Printed and bound in China by South China
Printing Company

ISBN 1 844 43283 1
09 08 07 06 05
10 9 8 7 6 5 4 3 2 1

**British Library Cataloguing in
Publication Data**
Bingham, Jane
Johnny Depp. – (Star Files)
791.4'3'028'092
A full catalogue record for this book is
available from the British Library.

Acknowledgements
The publishers would like to thank the
following for permission to reproduce
photographs: Allstar (Cinetext Collection)
pp. **4**, **9** (b), **17** (t), **20**, **21** (l), **23** (b), **23** (t),
25 (b), **30** (b), **31**, **38**; Allstar Collection pp.
15 (b), **32** (r), **33**, **39** (b); Allstarpl.com p. **21**
(r); Corbis pp. **9** (t) (Gianni Dagli Orti),
12 (SYGMA/Cardinale Stephane), **14**, **29**
(SYGMA/Picturescope Internat), **30** (Stapleton
Collection), **36** (Bettmann); Getty Images
(Photodisc) pp. **10** (t), **15** (t), **37**; iStockPhoto
pp. **7** (t) (Dan Brandenburg), **17** (b) (Allen
Johnson); Retna Ltd pp. **24** (Steve Granitz),
27 (Sara De Boer), **28** (t) (Robert Frazier),
32 (l) (Robert Matheu), **36** (r) (Carmen
Valdes); Rex Features pp. **5** (Vinnie Zuffante),
6 (Camilla Morandi), **7** (b) (Joyce Silverstein),
8 (Kip Rano), **10** (b) (Richard Young),
11 (Richard Young), **13** (Karl Schoendorfer),
16 (Ray Tang), **18** (SNAP), **19** (SNAP), **22** (Pic
Photos), **25** (t) (SNAP), **26** (SNAP), **28** (b)
(Crollalanza), **34**, **35** (Paul Grover), **39** (t),
40 (Nils Jorgensen), **41** (b) (Makey/Rooke), **41**
(t) (Peter Brooker), **42** (C. Warner Br/Everett),
43 (Peter Brooker).
Cover photograph reproduced with permission
of Rex Features (Vinnie Zuffante).

Quote sources: pp. **4**, **8**, **10**, **13**, **19**, **23**, **27**,
32, **34**, **38** *What's Eating Johnny Depp?* Nigel
Goodall, 2004; p. **29** http://www.ohjohnny.
net/quotes.html; pp. **37**, **42** Interview in *Time*
magazine, 15th March 2004.

The publishers would like to thank Rosie
Nixon, Charly Rimsa, Sarah Williams, Marie
Lorimer, and Nicola Hodgson for their
assistance in the preparation of this book.

Every effort has been made to contact
copyright holders of any material reproduced
in this book. Any omissions will be rectified
in subsequent printings if notice is given to
the publishers.

The paper used to print this book comes from
sustainable resources.

Disclaimer: This book is not authorized or
approved by Johnny Depp.

Johnny is photographed wherever he goes.

In which film does Johnny meet a headless horseman?

Which comedian is Johnny a fan of?

Which **director** has Johnny worked with four times?

Johnny the rebel

Johnny is not the usual kind of screen star. Despite his stunning looks, he hardly ever chooses glamorous roles. Instead, he often plays **oddball** characters. Johnny says he likes playing outsiders. He thinks that they are more like him.

Not just an actor

Acting is not Johnny's only interest. His first love is music. He says he wants his life to be filled with different experiences.

oddball unusual

Young Johnny

Family tattoos

Johnny has a Betty Sue tattoo on his left arm. It shows his mum's name inside a red heart. On his right arm is the name of his son, Jack. Over his heart is his daughter's name – Lily-Rose.

★ ★ ★ ★ ★ ★ ★ ★ ★ ★

Johnny spent his early years in the southern state of Kentucky, United States. His father was a city engineer in the town of Owensboro. His mother – Betty Sue – worked as a waitress in a local coffee shop.

The Depp family did not have a lot of money to spare. They lived in an ordinary house in an ordinary town, just like other families.

A close family

When he was growing up, Johnny was very close to his mother. He also spent as much time as he could with his grandfather. Johnny's special name for his grandfather was Pawpaw.

Young Johnny followed Pawpaw everywhere. He even worked beside him, picking crops in the fields. Johnny was only 7 years old when Pawpaw died. He missed his grandfather very badly.

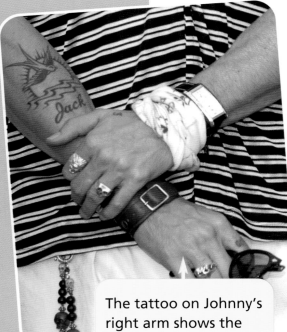

The tattoo on Johnny's right arm shows the name of his son.

Star fact

Johnny believes in ghosts. Sometimes he feels his grandfather's ghost watching over him.

Star words   Cherokee   member of a Native American people that used to live in most of the southern United States

Youngest in the family

Johnny was the youngest in his family. He has two half-sisters – Debbie and Christie – and a brother – Dan. Now, Christie and Dan both work with Johnny. Christie is Johnny's manager and adviser. Dan is Johnny's partner in a **film production company**.

Johnny used to help his grandfather pick crops in Kentucky.

Cherokee ancestors

Johnny's grandfather came from a Native American family. Pawpaw's ancestors belonged to the **Cherokee** tribe. Johnny's **dramatic** colouring and high cheekbones show that that he has Cherokee blood.

Johnny is still close to his mother.

film production company business that makes films to earn money

Daredevil hero

When Johnny was growing up, one of his heroes was Evel Knievel (below). Evel Knievel was a daring stuntman who performed amazing motorcycle jumps. Once, he jumped over a row of thirteen double-decker buses. Evel Knievel often crash-landed and broke many bones.

Moving to Florida

When Johnny was 8 years old, his family moved to Florida. His father John worked in Miramar, a small town north of Miami. The family did not like living in Miramar, but they had to stay there because of John's job.

Johnny's family never really settled in Miramar. They kept on moving from place to place. Most of the time, they lived in **motel** rooms.

All the Depp children were unhappy in Florida. Each time they moved house, they had to get to know a new group of friends. In the end, Johnny stopped trying to make new friends.

Odd one out

Johnny did not do well at school. He did not try in lessons and he was a **rebel** and a daredevil. He was also different from the other children.

❝ I was not the most popular kid at school. I always felt like a total freak. ❞

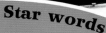

Star words

gospel type of music and songs sung in Christian churches
motel a roadside hotel for motorists

He hated most of the popular television shows. Instead he watched old films about the Second World War. He also spent a lot of time on his own, digging tunnels and thinking up "great escapes".

Learning from the preacher

On Sundays, Johnny's family went to hear his uncle preach at a nearby church. Johnny's uncle ran a popular **gospel** group. Johnny loved to watch his uncle stand up on the stage and perform. He decided that he would be a performer when he grew up.

This is a self-portrait of Van Gogh.

Johnny took ideas from films such as *The Great Escape*.

Wild artist

While Johnny was living in Florida, he became interested in Vincent Van Gogh. Van Gogh was a 19th-century painter who created a **dramatic** style of his own. Johnny admired Van Gogh for being a great artist, and also a rebel and a loner.

rebel someone who behaves differently from most other people

9

Getting into music

By the time he was 12 years old, Johnny felt his life was not going well. Then his mum bought him a special present. She spent US$25 on an electric guitar. From then on, Johnny spent hours locked in his bedroom. He was determined to learn to play the guitar.

Johnny taught himself to play by listening to records and repeating what he heard. His two favourite bands were the Sex Pistols and U2. The Sex Pistols were a leading punk rock group. U2 made a different type of music called "New Wave". Johnny's aim was to create a sound that was a blend of the two different styles.

> **"** All I wanted since I was 12 years old was to join a band and go on the road. **"**

Punk rock

Punk rock started in the late 1970s. It was meant to shock and even frighten people. Punk bands made loud, raw, angry music. Most of their songs were violent attacks on modern **society**.

The Sex Pistols were a famous punk band.

Star words   society all the different groups of people in a country

The Irish band U2 made songs with a powerful message.

Flame

Soon, Johnny was ready to form his own band. The band was called Flame and they wrote their own music. Most of the time they just practised in a garage, but sometimes they played a local gig. Later, the band changed their name to The Kids.

Johnny designed the costumes for Flame. At first, the band wore simple T-shirts that said Flame. Then they wore plain shirts. Then they started to wear more exciting costumes, such as crushed velvet shirts and bell-bottom trousers. Johnny found most of these clothes in his mother's wardrobe.

New Wave

New Wave music began at the same time as punk rock. It had a different sound from punk, but it still had a powerful message. Elvis Costello, Blondie, and Talking Heads were all part of the New Wave movement.

11

Iggy Pop

Iggy Pop is sometimes called the grandfather of punk rock. He began performing in the 1960s with his band The Stooges. He has also appeared in over fifteen films. Iggy had a small part in *Cry Baby*, one of Johnny's first films.

Johnny and Iggy Pop together at the Cannes Film Festival.

Tough times

When Johnny was fifteen, his parents divorced and the family split up. His father and sister Debbie moved to a different town. The rest of the family stayed with Betty Sue.

It was a very hard time for Johnny. He hated school. He also worried about his mum, who was very upset about the divorce. The one good thing in his life was his music. The Kids were starting to be a success. They had begun to play in the local clubs.

Star fact

When he played for The Kids, Johnny usually earned about US$25 a day. Now he can earn a thousand times that much.

Star words   **warm-up band** band that performs at the beginning of a gig – usually before a more famous band comes on stage

The Kids take off

At the age of sixteen, Johnny dropped out of school. He concentrated on writing songs and playing with The Kids. The band began to play in clubs all over Florida. Sometimes The Kids were the **warm-up band** for a famous music act. They played on the same stage as the B52s, Talking Heads, and Iggy Pop.

Early marriage

Around this time Johnny met Lori Allison. She was a make-up artist and a great fan of The Kids. Johnny and Lori fell in love. They got married when he was 20 and she was 25. Lori believed that The Kids had a great future. She worked very hard to try and help make the band a success.

Too young?

Looking back, Johnny thinks he got married too young. "I had the right intentions," he says, "but the wrong timing."

13

Starting out

★ ★ ★ ★ ★ ★ ★ ★ ★ ★

City of Angels

Los Angeles is not just famous for Hollywood. It is also a major music centre. Every year, hundreds of young bands arrive in LA. They all hope to get noticed by the city's record companies and **music producers**. Only a handful ever succeed.

★ ★ ★ ★ ★ ★ ★ ★ ★ ★

In 1984, The Kids moved to Los Angeles. They hoped that this was their chance to make it really big. Life was hard in LA, though. There were just too many bands trying to succeed.

Trying to survive

Life in Los Angeles was a struggle. The Kids were not a big success and there was not enough money to pay the bills. All the members of the band were forced to get other jobs. Johnny worked at lots of low-paid jobs.

It was also a hard time for Johnny and Lori. They both realized they were drifting apart. In the end, they agreed that it would be best to split up. The couple got divorced when Johnny was 22.

The Kids moved to Los Angeles to try and make it big!

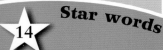

14

Star words

agent someone who works for actors or other performers and tries to find them jobs

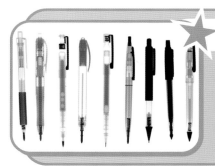

Star fact

For a few weeks, Johnny had a job selling ballpoint pens over the telephone.

A lucky break

Just before Johnny and Lori split up, they went to meet an old friend of Lori's. This friend was the actor Nicolas Cage. By that time, Nicolas had already been in lots of films.

Nicolas liked Johnny's spiky-haired, punk-rock image. He thought that Johnny would look good on screen. He suggested that Johnny should meet his **agent**. It was Johnny's first move into the world of acting.

Nicolas Cage

Nicolas Cage is one of Hollywood's leading actors. He has acted in comedies, thrillers, and action films. In 2002 he starred in *Adaptation* (below), where he played two parts – a **screenwriter** and his imaginary brother.

music producer someone who decides how a piece of music or a song will sound when it is being recorded

Jessica's choice

Wes Craven was not the only one to think that Johnny was right for his film. His teenage daughter Jessica was bowled over by Johnny's looks. She told her father he had to choose Johnny.

Oliver Stone is a very famous director. He has made many successful films.

A Nightmare on Elm Street

Thanks to Nicolas Cage, Johnny went to meet the film **director**, Wes Craven. He was making a horror film called *A Nightmare on Elm Street*. Craven was looking for someone to play the part of Glen Lantz. As soon as he saw Johnny, Craven knew he had found the right man. He could see that Johnny had star quality.

The next step

After *Nightmare*, Johnny had a couple of parts in television films. He also starred in a teen comedy – *Private Resort*. Johnny hated the film – and so did the **critics**. Around this time Johnny decided he needed some acting training, so he enrolled at the Loft Studio. This was a drama school where actors learnt techniques such as **voice control**. After his course at the Loft Johnny was a much better actor, but he still did not have much work.

Soldier boy

Then, one day, Johnny got a call from director Oliver Stone. Stone was planning a film about the Vietnam War, called *Platoon*. He thought that Johnny could play the young soldier, Private Lerner.

★ Star fact

In *Platoon*, Johnny wears a helmet with "Sherilyn" painted on it. At that time, he was dating the actress Sherilyn Fenn.

Star words

critics people who watch films, plays, and other shows and write what they think about them

Platoon was praised for showing the Vietnam War in a very realistic way.

Platoon is based on Oliver Stone's own experiences in Vietnam. It stars Charlie Sheen, Tom Berenger, and Willem Dafoe. Critics loved the film and praised Johnny's performance.

Jungle training

Oliver Stone is a brilliant, but tough, director. He made all the actors in *Platoon* train in the jungle for 2 weeks. The training included a 97-kilometre (60-mile) march. Many of the actors suffered from insect bites and fever.

Platoon was shot in thick jungle in the Philippine Islands.

voice control ways of making actors' voices stronger and clearer

Cops in schools

21 Jump Street was based on a real police experiment. In 1974, a group of officers pretended to be students in Los Angeles schools. They arrested several young drug dealers. Many people objected to the experiment, however, and it was dropped.

Officer Tom

Soon after he had finished filming *Platoon*, Johnny was offered a part in a television series. The series was *21 Jump Street*. It followed the adventures of a group of undercover detectives who worked in a US high school. The **director** wanted Johnny to play the part of Officer Tom Hanson – one of the leading young detectives.

Right from the start, Johnny was not keen to play Officer Tom. He hated the idea of detectives in schools. Johnny turned down the role twice, but the director kept asking him. In the end, Johnny decided he needed the work. He signed up for a series of thirteen episodes.

Teen idol

21 Jump Street was a huge success, and Johnny became a teenage **idol**. Girls all over the United States fell in love with Officer Tom. Every month Johnny's face appeared on the covers of teenage magazines.

> Johnny in character as Officer Tom.

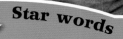

Star words   idol someone who is looked up to or admired by lots of people

He also got sack-loads of fan mail. None of this made Johnny happy, though. He hated being **idolized** for his looks.

Long-running show

Johnny stayed with *21 Jump Street* for 3 years. He even moved to Vancouver in Canada, where the series was being filmed. By the end of his 3 years, Johnny was very restless. He was desperate to try a more challenging role.

❝ I was this product. Teen Boy. Poster Boy. All that stuff that I wasn't. ❞

Fishy friend

When Johnny was filming *21 Jump Street*, he was visited by one of his few high-school friends, Sal Jenco. Sal did his usual trick of puffing out his cheeks like a blowfish. Sal was asked to join the show – and play a character called Blowfish.

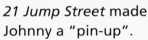

21 Jump Street made Johnny a "pin-up".

idolized worshipped, or loved

Jennifer co-starred with Patrick Swayze in the hit film *Dirty Dancing*.

Sherilyn and Jennifer

While he was working on *21 Jump Street*, Johnny got engaged twice. The first time was to actress Sherilyn Fenn. Sherilyn later starred in the television series *Twin Peaks*.

Johnny's second engagement was to Jennifer Grey. Jennifer played the lead in *Dirty Dancing*. The film was a great success, and made Jennifer a star.

Neither of Johnny's engagements lasted very long. Johnny had to spend long periods of time in Canada, filming *21 Jump Street*. This made it hard to hold a relationship together. Johnny was searching for the right woman – but he had not found her yet.

Return to the big screen

In 1989, **director** John Waters offered Johnny a great film role. He wanted Johnny to play the hero in his film *Cry Baby*. The film is set in the 1950s. It tells the story of Cry Baby Walker, a teenage heart-throb, who hangs around with a very bad crowd. Cry Baby only has to shed one tear to make all the girls fall in love with him. Johnny loved playing Cry Baby. It gave him the chance to get back into films. It also made fun of his real-life role as a teenage heart-throb.

John Waters

Johnny is a great fan of film director John Waters. Waters makes "bad taste" films that deal with trashy parts of **society**. His film *Hairspray* tells the story of a group of teenage **celebrities** and their mothers. It was also made into a hit musical.

Star words   celebrity famous person

James Dean lookalike

In his role as Cry Baby, Johnny reminded many people of another young star. James Dean (above) was a teenage **idol** in the 1950s. Just like Johnny, James Dean was famous for combining stunning good looks with great acting talent.

Johnny's looks made him perfect for the role of Cry Baby Walker.

Highs and lows

★ ★ ★ ★ ★ ★ ★ ★ ★ ★

Tim Burton

Tim Burton began his career by directing horror films. His first big break came when he directed the **black comedy** *Beetlejuice*. Many of Burton's films mix fantasy and comedy. *Batman* is one of his most famous films.

★ ★ ★ ★ ★ ★ ★ ★ ★ ★

In 1990, the **director** Tim Burton offered Johnny a very exciting role. He asked Johnny to star in his film, *Edward Scissorhands*. Burton had already made his name with the **blockbuster**, *Batman*. This meant he had plenty of money to spend. He wanted to make a spectacular film, and he wanted Johnny to be its star.

Strange story

Tim Burton had the idea for *Edward Scissorhands* when he was very young. He imagined the story of a strange inventor who created a boy with hedge-clipper hands. *Edward Scissorhands* is a brilliant mixture of dark fantasy and comedy. Some **critics** called it a modern fairy tale.

Films

Johnny has been in four Tim Burton films:

Edward Scissorhands (1988)

Ed Wood (1994)

Sleepy Hollow (1999)

Charlie and the Chocolate Factory (2005)

Johnny and Tim Burton enjoy working together.

Star words **black comedy** mixture of comedy with a serious, sometimes quite horrible, story

Great actors

Johnny was not the only star in *Edward Scissorhands*. The film also featured Vincent Price and Winona Ryder. Vincent was a famous horror actor, and he played Edward's weird inventor. Winona took the part of Kim – the girl who falls in love with Edward. At the time that they were filming *Edward Scissorhands*, Johnny and Winona were dating. This could have been awkward, but Tim Burton says it was never a problem. "They were very **professional**," he says. "They didn't bring any weird stuff to the set."

Sad hero

Johnny loved playing Edward Scissorhands. He was **fascinated** by the idea of a character who "wants to touch but can't".

Boris Karloff played Frankenstein's monster in a famous old film of the story.

★ ★ ★ ★ ★ ★ ★ ★ ★ ★

Monsters?

Edward Scissorhands has a connection with the tale of Frankenstein. In both stories, a weird inventor gives life to a strange creature. Frankenstein's creation is always seen as a monster. Edward is kind-hearted, but his strange appearance means that people are afraid of him.

★ ★ ★ ★ ★ ★ ★ ★ ★ ★

fascinated   very interested
professional   focused on work

Winona Ryder

Winona Ryder made her name as an actress in the **black comedy**, *Beetlejuice*. She likes to take challenging roles and has starred in such varied films as *Little Women* and *Girl, Interrupted*.

Johnny and Winona

Johnny and Winona first met in 1989. Winona was only 17 years old, but she had already been in several films. Johnny was 26. They were both talented and good-looking – and they clicked immediately.

After they had been dating for 5 months, Johnny gave Winona an engagement ring. A month later, they were living together. They tried to spend as much time together as they could, but they did not plan to marry straight away.

Johnny and Winona were photographed everywhere they went.

⭐ Star fact

Johnny once sent Winona 200 helium balloons. They filled a whole room!

Most of the time, Johnny and Winona were very happy, but sometimes things got difficult. They both worked very long hours, and everywhere they went they were followed by the press.

In the end, the pressures got too much. They also began to realize that they were drifting apart. By 1993, Johnny's relationship with Winona was over.

Star words   dropout someone who does not fit in easily with other people

New directions

Around the time that Johnny and Winona were splitting up, Johnny accepted another unusual film role. He was ready for a new challenge in his acting career.

Benny and Joon

In the film *Benny and Joon*, Johnny plays Sam – a strange, clown-like character. Sam is a **dropout** who cannot read. He expresses himself by performing silent comedy acts.

Sam's acts are based on the silent films of Buster Keaton. Johnny studied these films for hours on end. He tried out all Keaton's tricks and falls – and ended up with lots of bruises!

Silent star

Buster Keaton (above) was one of the greatest stars of silent films. Like Charlie Chaplin, he acted in comedy films – getting into endless scrapes. Buster had trained as an acrobat and did all his own stunts.

The character of Sam gets into some scrapes performing his comedy acts!

Gilbert Grape

After *Benny and Joon*, Johnny's next major film was *What's Eating Gilbert Grape?* In this film, Johnny plays the part of Gilbert – a young man stuck in a small town.

Gilbert has a dead-end job and a problem family to support. His mother is extremely overweight and never leaves the house. His father is dead, and his brother, Arnie, has serious problems that affect his behaviour.

Into this unhappy life comes young Becky. She offers Gilbert the chance to escape. In the end, he has to choose between his family and his freedom.

Small town life

The town of Endora in *Gilbert Grape* does not really exist, but it is typical of thousands of small US towns. Johnny knows this kind of town very well. He has compared Endora to the town of Miramar, where he grew up.

Gilbert tries to take care of his brother Arnie, played by Leonardo DiCaprio.

26

Star words   **campaigning** trying hard to make something happen, or change something

Playing himself?

Some people say that Johnny played himself when he played Gilbert. Johnny does not agree, but he does admit that there are "**parallels**" between his life and Gilbert's. After his parents split up, Johnny had to look after his mother. They had very little money and he felt trapped in a boring town. "Sometimes you play roles that you are close to," says Johnny, "you **identify** with the guy."

Young Leo

Leonardo DiCaprio played the part of Gilbert's brother. Leo was 19 years old when he played Arnie. He had been appearing in films since he was fourteen.

During filming, Leo and Johnny spent a lot of time together. Later, Leo said it was just like being brothers.

> Johnny's hard to figure out. But that makes him interesting. (Leonardo DiCaprio)

Leonardo DiCaprio

After he appeared in *Gilbert Grape*, Leonardo DiCaprio's film career took off. In 2 years he was playing the lead in *Romeo and Juliet*. Now Leo (below) has made many successful films. He also spends time **campaigning** to save the environment.

identify recognize or relate to
parallels things that are similar or the same

Johnny and Kate

A few months after Johnny and Winona split up, Johnny met English supermodel Kate Moss in a New York cafe. They started to go out together almost immediately. Even though Johnny was 11 years older than Kate, they got on really well. Johnny liked Kate's English sense of humour, and they had a lot of fun together.

At that time, photos of Kate were everywhere. This did not mean that Kate was big-headed, though. Johnny loved the fact that she was so down-to-earth.

★ ★ ★ ★ ★ ★ ★ ★ ★ ★ ★

Kate Moss

Kate Moss is one of the world's best-known fashion models. She is famous for her striking, **waiflike** looks and her boyish figure. Kate has worked for all the big designers, including Calvin Klein and Yves Saint Laurent.

★ ★ ★ ★ ★ ★ ★ ★ ★ ★ ★

Kate and Johnny made a stunning couple.

Star words   waiflike very thin

Stormy scenes

Kate and Johnny had a stormy relationship. Sometimes they had big arguments and separated for a while. Then they got back together again and everything was fine. One major problem for Johnny and Kate was the press. Photographers loved to spot the glamorous couple. Several times, Johnny lost his temper with them.

One night, Johnny had a disagreement with a security guard at the hotel where he was staying. Johnny got so worked up that he trashed a hotel room. He was arrested and held in a cell for 48 hours. This was a low point in his life. Later, he tried to explain, "I'm human and I get angry like everybody else."

Weird roles?

Over the next few years, Johnny kept on working hard. Most of the parts he played were **oddball** characters. Usually the **critics** loved his films, but not everyone was impressed. Some people thought he should stop picking such weird roles.

" I just do the roles I like. I hate the obvious stuff. I don't respond to it. "

Fairy-tale house

While he was going out with Kate, Johnny found an amazing house (below). It looked like a fairy-tale castle. Johnny knew straightaway he had to buy it. Now it is his home whenever he works in Hollywood.

Johnny the star

In the late 1990s, Johnny played some very popular roles. He kept on playing unusual characters, but some of his films appealed to more people than before.

Sleepy Hollow

One of the big film successes of 1999 was *Sleepy Hollow*. The film *Sleepy Hollow* is based on a famous story by Washington Irving. Tim Burton **directed** the film and it was Johnny's third film with him.

In *Sleepy Hollow*, Johnny plays Constable Ichabod Crane. He is sent to investigate a murder committed by a headless horseman. For most of the film, Crane is scared out of his mind. It is the kind of role that Johnny really enjoys. He gave a very exciting performance.

Washington Irving

The American author Washington Irving (above) lived from 1783 to 1859. As well as writing *The Legend of Sleepy Hollow* he also wrote the tale of Rip Van Winkle, a man who slept for 20 years.

Constable Crane is a bit of an **oddball**!

Star words   soundtrack   music for a film

French actress Juliette Binoche played opposite Johnny in *Chocolat*.

Chocolat

The year after *Sleepy Hollow* appeared, Johnny took a minor role in the film *Chocolat*.

⭐ **Star fact**

Johnny plays the first and last songs on the **soundtrack** for *Chocolat*.

In this light-hearted film, he plays a travelling guitar player. Johnny only appears on screen for 17 minutes, but some people think he is the star of the film.

Some of Johnny's fans were surprised that he chose such a romantic part, but the character obviously appealed to him. It also gave him the chance to play his guitar on screen.

Chocolate roles

Chocolat is not Johnny's only film featuring chocolate. He also plays Willy Wonka – the owner of the factory in *Charlie and the Chocolate Factory*. Luckily, Johnny loves chocolate. He is especially keen on milk chocolate footballs.

Pirates of the Caribbean

So far, Johnny's most **high-profile** role is Captain Jack Sparrow from *Pirates of the Caribbean*. The film is based on a Disneyland ride and is aimed at all ages. One of the reasons Johnny chose to star in *Pirates* was because his children could enjoy watching the film.

Keith Richards

Keith Richards (above) is a good friend of Johnny's. He has been in the Rolling Stones since 1962. Now, Johnny has persuaded Keith to try acting as well. Keith will play Captain Jack's father in the sequel to *Pirates*.

Johnny's performance as Captain Jack was very unusual – but it worked!

Johnny's daughter Lily-Rose was 4 years old when he made *Pirates*. Johnny took her to watch him filming some of the scenes. Johnny says that Lily-Rose loved his costume. "She really liked the teeth and all the stuff dangling in my hair," he says. "She thinks her daddy is a real pirate."

Star words   high-profile getting lots of attention

Captain Jack

Pirates of the Caribbean is a classic storybook adventure, but Captain Jack is not the usual storybook pirate. Johnny based the character of Captain Jack on Keith Richards of the Rolling Stones.

Finding Neverland

Pirates of the Caribbean is not Johnny's only film featuring pirates. In *Finding Neverland*, Johnny plays James Barrie, the author of *Peter Pan*. The film shows how Barrie got his ideas for the story of Peter and the scary pirate Captain Hook.

 Star fact

Johnny was **nominated** for an Oscar for his roles as Captain Jack Sparrow and James Barrie.

Rejected roles

Johnny always insists that he is not "blockbuster boy". Here are a few of the big roles that he has turned down:

Robin Hood in Robin Hood Prince of Thieves (taken by Kevin Costner)

Lestat in Interview with a Vampire (taken by Tom Cruise)

Dracula in Bram Stoker's Dracula (taken by Gary Oldman)

Officer Jack Traven in Speed (taken by Keanu Reeves)

Johnny plays at being a pirate as James Barrie in *Finding Neverland*.

Family life

Vanessa the musician

Vanessa Paradis was born in Paris, France, and first shot to fame when she was only 14 years old. In 1986, her song, "*Joe le Taxi*", became an international hit. Over the next 6 years, she made 3 albums. In 2000, Vanessa released a new album called *Bliss*.

Johnny is now in a happy, long-term relationship with Vanessa Paradis. The couple first met in 1998 while Johnny was filming in Paris. Johnny spotted Vanessa in a hotel. He asked her to join him at his table. A few months later, they were sharing a flat in Paris.

Johnny was thirty-five and had reached a stage in his life when he wanted to settle down. He dreamed of having children of his own. When he met Vanessa, Johnny soon discovered that she shared his dream.

Vanessa Paradis

Vanessa is a singer, an actress, and a model. She released her first hit song when she was just fourteen. At the age of seventeen, she made her first film. Over the next 10 years she appeared in 4 more films. By the time Vanessa met Johnny, she had also made her mark in the fashion world. In 1991, she became the new face for a famous perfume.

Lily-Rose and Jack

In May 1999 Johnny and Vanessa had their first child. They named her Lily-Rose Melody. Their son Jack was born

> They say life begins at 40, but for me it began at 35. That was the year I started my family.

3 years later. Johnny says that having children is the best thing that ever happened to him.

John Christopher Depp III

Johnny's son is named John Christopher Depp III, after his father and grandfather. Nobody ever calls him John, though. He is always known as Jack.

★ ★ ★ ★ ★ ★ ★ ★ ★ ★ ★

Vanessa and Johnny keep their children away from the press, but the couple are often seen out together.

Family first

Johnny tries to spend as much time as he can with Vanessa and his children. Most of all, he likes to stay at home – having fun with Lily-Rose and Jack.

Johnny and Vanessa have three homes – a flat in Paris, a house in Hollywood, and a house in the south of France. Usually they live in France. The Depp family home is a large villa in the French countryside, close to St Tropez.

Harry Houdini

The great magician Harry Houdini (above) lived from 1874 to 1926. Houdini was famous for his daring escape acts. He could even escape from a locked trunk placed under water. Johnny has always been **fascinated** by Houdini.

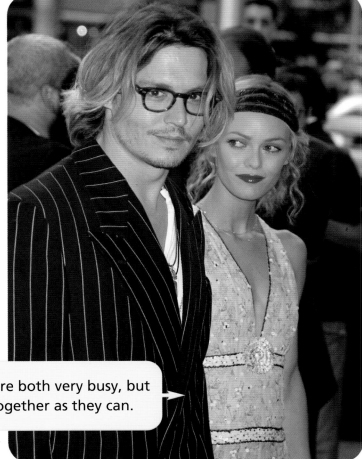

Johnny and Vanessa are both very busy, but spend as much time together as they can.

People from the local village often see Johnny shopping in the market. Johnny sometimes stops for a chat and his French is now quite good. Sometimes Johnny joins the old men of the village for a friendly game of *boules*, a game that is a bit like bowls.

66 These days, I just play Barbies and hang out with the kiddies. 99

Staying private

Johnny is determined to keep his family life out of the public eye. He wants his children to have a happy childhood – without the attention of the press.

Johnny the collector

Johnny loves collecting things. In the past, he used to keep lizards and snakes. Nowadays, he mainly collects paintings and old books. Johnny also has a collection of old locks. He started collecting locks after he got interested in the magician, Houdini.

Some of the things that Johnny collects are quite weird. He used to have a model of a life-sized yellow gorilla.

Likes/dislikes

Johnny likes:
Bugs
Snakes
Lizards
Funny hats

Johnny dislikes:
Spiders
Clowns

Other interests

Playing for Oasis

In 1997, Johnny played a **slide guitar** solo on the song "Fade In-Out" on the Oasis album *Be Here Now*. Noel Gallagher asked Johnny to play it for him because it was too hard for Noel to play himself.

Johnny's first love has always been music. Ever since he was 12 years old, he has played the guitar. Johnny formed his first band when he was thirteen – and he still plays in a band today.

Johnny has many friends in the music business. One of his friends is Noel Gallagher, from the band Oasis. Johnny also loves to play his guitar with Keith Richards of the Rolling Stones.

> I never really wanted to be an actor ... I was a musician and still am.

Johnny got to play the guitar in the film *Chocolat*.

Star words corrupt dishonest

A band called "P"

In 1993 Johnny and some friends formed a band called P. Other famous members include Flea from the Red Hot Chilli Peppers and Johnny's old friend Sal Jenco. The band still plays together whenever they can. In 1995 they released their first album.

Johnny gave his friend Noel Gallagher a white guitar with the letter "P" on it. Noel often uses this guitar at Oasis gigs.

Noel Gallagher of Oasis asked Johnny to play on their album.

Soundtracks

In 2003 Johnny wrote part of the music **soundtrack** for *Once upon a Time in Mexico* (below). In this film, Johnny plays the part of a **corrupt** CIA agent. Johnny wrote the haunting theme tune for his character.

More music

Johnny has appeared in lots of music videos. He played alongside Iggy Pop in one of his recent gigs. He has also **directed** several music videos for Vanessa Paradis.

On Vanessa's album, *Bliss*, Johnny plays lead guitar on two of the tracks. He also wrote the album's title song with Vanessa.

Fast laughs

Some of Johnny's best roles have been comic creations. He loves **quirky**, "off-the-wall" comedy. His all-time favourite television show is the British comedy, *The Fast Show*. *The Fast Show* only lasted for three series, but millions of people loved its crazy characters.

The last laugh

Johnny used to take tapes of *The Fast Show* with him when he was filming. He has become great friends with Paul Whitehouse, one of the show's creators and stars. Johnny appeared on the last ever sketch of *The Fast Show*. He played himself in a comic sketch called "Suits you". Paul Whitehouse appeared with Johnny again – this time on the big screen. He has a small part in the film *Finding Neverland*.

Johnny is a big fan of comedian Paul Whitehouse.

Star words   jet set people who have a lot of money and who often fly from one country to another

Star fact

Johnny loves Dr Seuss's *Cat in the Hat*. He says the Cat got him started on wearing funny hats.

Mister Stench

Johnny has always had an **offbeat** sense of humour. When he was 8 years old, he chose the nickname "Mister Stench" for himself.

A modest star

Johnny is asked to appear on celebrity shows all the time, but he almost always says no. He only takes part in things that he really believes in.

A restaurant in Paris

Today, Johnny is branching out in other directions. With his actor friends, Sean Penn and John Malkovich, he has bought a restaurant in Paris. The restaurant is called the Man Ray after a famous photographer, painter, and sculptor. It has become a favourite with the Paris **jet set**.

Like his choice of roles, Johnny's sense of style is pretty unusual.

offbeat unusual – not what people expect
quirky strange, or funny

New directions

Johnny the director

In 1996 Johnny directed *The Brave* – a story of a Native American. He also wrote the script with his brother Dan. *The Brave* was not a success, but some **critics** said that Johnny should try directing again.

★ ★ ★ ★ ★ ★ ★ ★ ★ ★

Charlie and the Chocolate Factory is a film that Johnny's children can watch and enjoy.

What does the future hold for Johnny? He wants to widen his range of roles. He has tried film **directing** once, and he will probably try it again. He will certainly stay involved in the world of music. Only one thing is certain – he will keep surprising everyone.

Different roles

Johnny plans to make more films that his children can enjoy. He plays the mad inventor, Willy Wonka, in *Charlie and the Chocolate Factory*. He will also return as Captain Jack Sparrow in *Pirates of the Caribbean 2: Dead Man's Chest*.

> I miss Captain Jack. I'm looking forward to meeting him again.

Star words   paralyzed unable to move

Johnny's voice will soon be heard in an animated film – *The Corpse Bride*. Meanwhile, he has taken on a challenging role in *The Diving Bell and the Butterfly*. In this unusual film, Johnny will play a totally **paralyzed** patient, who visits imaginary places in his mind.

Future awards?

During his career Johnny has been **nominated** for four Golden Globe awards. He has also been nominated for two Oscars – one for his role in *Pirates of the Caribbean* and the other for *Finding Neverland*. So far, though, Johnny has not won any of these big awards.

Surely this will change in the future. Sooner or later, Hollywood must recognize the **unique** talents of Johnny Depp.

Johnny has already been honoured with a star on the Walk of Fame in Hollywood.

unique only one

Find out more

Books to read
Depp, Christopher Heard (ECW Press, 2001)
Johnny Depp: The Biography, Nigel Goodall
    (Blake Publishing, 1999)
Johnny Depp: A Modern Rebel, Brian J. Robb
    (Plexus, 2004)
Johnny Depp: Movie Top Ten, Jack Hunter
    (Creation Publishing Group, 2000)
Johnny Depp: People in the News, Kara Higgins
    (Lucent Books, 2004)
What's Eating Johnny Depp? An Intimate Biography,
    Nigel Goodall (Blake Publishing, 2004)

Filmography
Charlie and the Chocolate Factory (2005)
Secret Window (2004)
The Libertine (2004)
Finding Neverland (2004)
Once Upon a Time in Mexico (2003)
Pirates of the Caribbean: the Curse of the Black Pearl
    (2003)
Lost in LaMancha (2002)
From Hell (2001)
Blow (2001)
Chocolat (2000)
Before Night Falls (2000)
The Man who Cried (2000)
Sleepy Hollow (1999)
The Ninth Gate (1999)
The Astronaut's Wife (1999)
Fear and Loathing in Las Vegas (1998)
LA Without a Map (1998)
Cannes Man (1996)
The Brave (1996)
Donnie Brasco (1996)
Nick of Time (1995)
Dead Man (1995)
Don Juan DeMarco (1995)
Ed Wood (1994)
Benny and Joon (1993)

What's Eating Gilbert Grape? (1993)
Arizona Dream (1991)
Freddy's Dead: The Final Nightmare (1991)
Cry Baby (1990)
Edward Scissorhands (1990)
21 Jump Street (Television series, 1987–1990)
Platoon (1986)
Private Resort (1985)
Nightmare on Elm Street (1984)

Music videos and albums

Que fait la vie? by Vanessa Paradis (director) (2001)
Pourtant by Vanessa Paradis (director) (2001)
"Fade In-Out" track on *Be Here Now* album by
  Oasis (1997)
"That Woman's Got Me Drinking" by Shane McGowan
  and the Pogues (guest appearance and director) (1994)
"Stuff" by John Frusciante (director) (1993)
"It's a Shame about Ray" by Lemonheads
  (guest appearance) (1991)
"Into the Great Wide Open" by Tom Petty
  (guest appearance) (1991)
"Joey" by Concrete Blond (guest appearance) (1990)

Websites

To find out more about Johnny Depp and his films, try
these websites:
http://www.johnnydeppfan.com
A fan club website for Johnny. Includes latest news,
pictures, and interviews.
http://www.ohjohnny.net/fast/fast.html
Shots of Johnny appearing in *The Fast Show*.

Disclaimer

All the Internet addresses (URLs) given in this book were valid at the time of
going to press. However, due to the dynamic nature of the Internet, some
addresses may have changed, or sites may have ceased to exist since
publication. While the author and publishers regret any inconvenience this
may cause readers, no responsibility for any such changes can be accepted by
either the author or the publishers.

Glossary

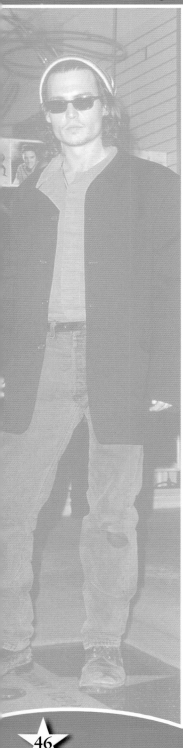

agent someone who works for actors or other performers and tries to find them jobs

black comedy mixture of comedy with a serious, sometimes quite horrible, story

blockbuster film that does really well at the cinema and earns lots of money

campaigning trying hard to make something happen, or change something

celebrity famous person

Cherokee member of a Native American people that used to live in most of the southern United States

corrupt dishonest

critics people who watch films, plays, and other shows and write what they think about them

director person in charge of making a film

dramatic striking; something that stands out

dropout someone who does not fit in easily with other people

fascinated very interested

film production company business that makes films to earn money

gospel type of music and songs sung in Christian churches

high-profile getting lots of attention

identify recognize or relate to

idol someone who is looked up to or admired by lots of people

idolized worshipped, or loved

jet set people who have a lot of money and who often fly from one country to another

motel a roadside hotel for motorists

music producer someone who decides how a piece of music or a song will sound when it is being recorded

nominated chosen as one of the people who might win an award

oddball unusual

offbeat unusual – not what people expect

parallels things that are similar or the same

paralyzed unable to move

professional focused on work

quirky strange, or funny

rebel someone who behaves differently from most
other people

screenwriter someone who writes the stories, or scripts, for
films and television shows

slide guitar style of guitar playing. The guitarist wears a piece
of metal (called a bottleneck) on their finger and slides this
over the strings to make a new sound.

society all the different groups of people in a country

soundtrack music for a film

unique only one

voice control ways of making actors' voices stronger
and clearer

waiflike very thin

warm-up band band that performs at the beginning of a gig –
usually before a more famous band comes on stage

Index

Titles in the *Star File* series include:

Johnny Depp
Jane Bingham
Hardback   1 844 43283 1

Beyoncé Knowles
Mark Stewart
Hardback   1 844 43296 3

Jackie Chan
Dan Fox
Hardback   1 844 43295 5

Usher
Dan Whitcombe
Hardback   1 844 43298 X

David Beckham
Paul Harrison
Hardback   1 844 43297 1

Andre Benjamin
Brian Fitzgerald
Hardback   1 844 43972 0

Mary-Kate and Ashley Olsen
Stephanie Fitzgerald
Hardback   1 410 91662 6

Orlando Bloom
Kay Barnham
Hardback   1 844 43284 X

Find out about other titles in this series on our website www.raintreepublishers.co.uk

TEDDY
and
The Seaside Holiday

Teddy was happy and filled with glee,
Today, they were going to Sunbury-on-Sea.
In a cottage by the sea, they were going to stay,
This was the start of their summer holiday.

Their bags were packed with all they would need,
     Including buckets, spades and books to read.
Daddy Bear started his bright red car,
     And off they went, with a loud hurrah!

They had a cottage,
      With their cousins to share.
Excited and happy,
      They longed to be there.
On they drove,
      Not stopping for tea,
And at last they arrived,
      At Sunbury-on-Sea.

The other bears had only just arrived too,
     And the sun shone down, from a sky of blue.
They hurriedly put their swimming costumes on,
     Then off to the beach they were very soon gone.

They swam and splashed,
    In the bright shining sea,
Then dried off with towels,
    And went home for tea.

The grown-up bears had been busy indeed,
    And on brown bread and honey they began to feed.

There were fresh fruit, nuts,
    And lots to eat,
Being on holiday,
    Was certainly a treat.

Soon they were full,
    And the tired little bears,
Said, ''Goodnight,'' to their parents,
    And went upstairs.

Each had a bed,
  In the room at the top,
After brushing their teeth,
  'Neath the sheets did hop.
Teddy and Jimbo,
  Were soon fast asleep,
But Bessy and Belle,
  To the window did creep.

They looked out upon a silvery sea,
     And there in the moonlight a tall ship did see.
It was close to the shore, and a light flashed near by,
     ''Keep clear of the rocks,'' it seemed to cry.

Suddenly from the ship, a small boat they saw,
   Some Sailor Bears were rowing hard for the shore.
They jumped in the surf, giving each other a hand,
   Then hauled their boat up onto the sand.

They lit a fire and dried their feet,
    Then all sat down and began to eat.
They sang, ''Yo ho ho, how happy are we,
    It's a good life for a bear when he's sailing the sea!''

Bessy and Belle were feeling sleepy at last,
  And looking at the clock, saw it was midnight past.
So they slipped into their nice warm beds,
  And snuggled deep down their furry heads.

At breakfast next day,
    They told what they had seen,
But Teddy and Jimbo said,
    "It might be a dream."
So they went to the beach,
    And looked at the sand.
In the remains of the fire,
    They found a gold band.

"Pirates' gold, that's what it must be,"
    Said Teddy, with great authority.
They cleaned off the ash and inside did look,
    And all together read, "Captain Hook."

Just as they were wondering what to do,
        Bosun Bear came into view.
"I'm the keeper of the lighthouse,"
        He told the bears,
"And I've just walked down,
        Three hundred stairs."

"I've had a signal from Captain Hook,
        He's lost his ring and I've come to look."
"We've found it, we've found it,"
        All the bears cried out.
"Well blow me down," said Bosun,
        "There's no need to shout."

"I'll signal the Captain in Plymouth Sound,
     He'll be very pleased that his ring has been found.
There's sure to be a reward for you young bears,
     So it's back to the lighthouse and climbing those stairs."

Captain Hook and his crew returned next day,
　　　They were glad they hadn't sailed too far away.
"It was careless of me to let my ring slip free.
　　　You must be my guests and spend a day on the sea."

The bears rushed home,
    Their parents to bring,
And tell them all about,
    Captain Hook's ring.
They sailed the sea,
    For the rest of the day,
Then in the evening,
    Returned to the bay.

Captain Hook said, "We must do this again,
But now we're off to the Spanish Maine.
Goodbye my hearties and be of good cheer,
I'll see you again; same time next year!"